Bill Green

Spoof

poems and parodies

Entire Photo Here Press

ISBN   0-9529685-1-7
         978-0-9529685-1-1

First published 2005 by
Entire Photo Here Press
The Cottage
Chulmleigh Road
Morchard Bishop
Devon EX17 6NZ

Copies of the book are available post free from the above address.

Acknowledgements. Thanks are due to the editors of the following magazines and newspapers in which most of these pieces first appeared: *New Statesman*, *The Independent*, *The Spectator*, *The Literary Review*, *NATE News*, *EDAT News*. "Johnny Simpson" and "Postman Pat" were commissioned by BBC Radio 4. "Coochi-Coochi" first appeared in *This Poem Doesn't Rhyme*, ed. Gerard Benson (Viking). I'm grateful to Fatboy, Spiro Keats, Fat Jeff, Babe Bio, Ms de Meaner, and the many other New Statesman comp commandants over the last 30 years; and to Boyd Tonkin.

Printed in Great Britain by Short Run Press,
25 Bittern Road, Sowton, Exeter, Devon.

This book is dedicated to El Basilio

Contents

Also by Bill Greenwell:
Tony Blair Reminds Me Of A Budgie (Entire Photo Here, 1996)
Impossible Objects (Cinnamon Press, 2006)

Visit the web-site www.billgreenwell.com for the entire text of *Tony Blair Reminds Me Of A Budgie,* and many other *New Statesman* poems. Visit www.theweeklypoem.com for a weekly satirical poem.
Contact by e-mail: billgreenwellcwr@aol.com

A View Of Ted Hughes (by the pig)

The man stood with his biro poised.
He was paid, they said, as much as three men.
His jutting jaw, thick furrowed eyebrows.
These jotters stand straight out.

His gait and native Yorkshire grit
Seemed to me a bloody cheek.
I was just a dead porker, not yet sliced.
And he wanted his pound of flesh.

He clocked me one with his fist.
It did not seem to bother him,
Smacking my crackling. His kind
Are always coining it with animals.

Even bacon deserves a bit of respect.
That includes bluff, gruff Northern sorts.
This git in the old leather jacket,
How would he like to be soused in hot water?

Gerard Manley Hopkins rewrites *Three Blind Mice*

Ah, see, see! the sightless, the flight fleet
  Of squealing squeakers, a wisp-whiskered trinity:
   How needless, heedless of wife's knife's vicinity,
Throat-threatening, they run than rather retreat!
Now tails trimmed, a timorous trio's feet
  Come tip-tumbling in marvellous, mewling affinity
   Of mice! In a trice, with One-in-Three divinity,
They chase the chopper, which lightly lopped each seat!

And what harvester, reaper, weeps not at such horrible halving,
  When lengths, limp, lie strength-ended, and behind
Is bare, each stropped, stripped, cropped by her carving?
  How hard is the farm-mistress' arm to their harmless kind:
For the fast-footed, fated field-mice, parlour-bent, were starving,
  Thieving for a cheese, for a rind, yet ah! were all blind!

Carol Ann Duffy: *Once In Royal David's City*

It was in that city. You could see
that David had been there, right royal
except for drizzle on the paving.
Evening like dull pain. Stranger. Manger.
Straw for the mother to deliver
a message from heaven. The poor,
the mean, and the moody. She was Mary,
and the kid arriving at half-seven.

Christ. Jesus. Messiah. His new skin
crinkling in starlight. The local oxen
paddled their tongues by the crib,
dunking their thick heads in shadow.
It was holy all right. You could taste
the dew in his ducts, hear his gurgle
like a broken tap. His maiden mother
was as gentle as Carnation. Or Lux.

Birth was a redemption, a revelation
of good. Ace. Perfect. Brill. Bright.
Love. Faith. The whisper of a child
is like the rustle of feed. You look on
and this is no playpen, no stable.
Weak and helpless. No, he was going
up in the world. Angel. A bright spark
born in a stall. God's gift. No kidding.

Taking Pepsi with Fiona Pitt-Kethley

Once I had Pepsi with Pitt-Kethley -
she liked my bottle, so she told me.
It was curvaceous, with a slender neck.

Men like me like their bottles knobbly,
(so Fiona says). They jack the tops off
to slug back the brown, artificial
bubbles - then tell her something reminds
them of something... and once cost 1/3.

Pepsi gets right up Fiona's nostrils.
She jerked mine clean across the formica
and mouthed obscenities over its rim,
slurping the cola with thrusting lips.

"Pepsi sucks, but I prefer Coke,"
Fiona told me, fondling the bottle
into a nearby bin. She looked practised.

I can have a drink on her any time, Fiona said.

The Hollow Men by William Blake

A Scarecrow with his Head of Straw
Is fill'd with Nothing evermore.
The Blind Man's dreams are full at Night
Of those in Heaven still with Sight.
The Dullard wakening to Despair
Has Thoughts composed of empty Air.
The Fools that by a Cactus pray
Shall never kiss at break of Day.
The Crowd upon the hopeless Beach
See Rose & Star they ne'er can reach.
He who hears the Five Bells chime
Shall chant a final Nursery Rhyme.
A Shadow falling here and there
Defeats Man's Memory of Prayer.
A quiet not a violent Noise
Proves the end of this World's Joyes.

The Day Of The Jackal by **John Motson**

and here's the Jackal he's
oh wellplayed there's nothing this man can't tackle
sun shining high in the sky as he slips past his shadow

fine player this and he's been

oh lovely dummy bought by the club to cause a bit
a bit of a stir on the right wing
feints neatly there

the Jackal

has small arms and they're already putting
a huge price on his head
plays a very deep game
the opposition is calling him all sorts of names
but they can't put him off

he's dashing
oh yes he squeezed through that gap
fantastic

every time they put a marker on him
he just shrugs it off

this could be a very tight corner

perfect control of his balls

he's really motoring towards the target
they've got him they've got him no they haven't
this man is not putting a foot wrong

this the Jackal who

he's killed that one dead oh what skill
he's putting a new act together this is tremendous stuff and oh
he has so many weapons up his sleeve and it's Jackal again

uses his head
swerves
I think they've lost him
lost the Jackal

he's aiming in the right direction but they're
gunning for him but he passes

passes

passes and OH HE'S TAKING A LONG SHOT AT DE GAULLE

oh

and he's missed he's missed they're not going to be able to
   work out how now are they Trevor

Postman Pat Goes Kaput

It was a cloudy sort of day in Greendale. Postman Pat was at the post office very early.

"Hello, Mrs. Goggins," said Pat. "Is there anything for me to take up to Thompson Ground today?"

"Well," said Mrs. Goggins, "there were two letters, but they've been taken up by Mailman Max and Letterbox Len."

"Oh dear," said Pat. "Are there no birthday cards for the twins at Greendale Farm? It is their birthday, after all."

Mrs. Goggins sighed. "I'm very sorry, Pat," she said, "but they text-messaged me only five minutes ago. All their cards and presents are being popped down their chimney by Airmageddon, the new helicopter service."

"My goodness," said Pat. "They'll have to be careful. It's very high up there in the sky. It'll be what they call a real mail drop."

"The Reverend Timms did call in," said Mrs. Goggins. "He asked if you could collect the parish magazines."

Pat was on his way. "Cheerio!" he said.

"Not so fast," said Mrs. Goggins. "Miss Hubbard was here as well, and it turns out that she has the vicarage concession with Churchround UK. She took the magazines on her bike. And Sam Waldron is delivering all the letters about winning through to the final stage of the Reader's Digest draw."

"Was I one of them?" said Pat.

"I'm very sorry," said Mrs. Goggins.

Just then, Ted Glen came into the post office. He was wearing a bright red and gold uniform and braided cap.

"Hello," said Pat. "You look very smart. Have you joined the brass band in Pencaster?"

"Not at all," said Ted. "I've joined Livery Delivery. We take round all the big parcels to the farms. I've got some tractor parts here. Would you like to see them?"

"Don't bother on my account," said Pat. He walked outside, and looked at the eleven post-boxes along the road, every one with a different colour. "My goodness," said Pat to Jess, who was curled up inside the van. "This is a first class service. It's a good job they broke the monopoly."

But Jess, purring quietly, jumped from his seat. He had a tag round his neck which read CommPet. He ran into the post office.

"Pat!" shouted Mrs. Goggins from inside. "There's a letter just arrived for you!"

"I'm on my way," said Pat. Jess came out of the door very shiftily. "A letter!" said Pat. "That's grand! I'll get the sack."

Mrs. Goggins gave him an envelope. "I think you've got it already," she said.

JOHNNY SIMPSON *and the Gates of Kabul*

Johnny wasn't terribly sure what to do next. He knew that the Taleban shapes by the side of the road weren't moving, but that it still might not be safe. So he walked ahead of the Northern Alliance tanks, half wishing that he had not left his Invisibility Burqa back in Islamabad, heading for the shimmering city in the distance.

The first thing Johnny saw was a huge crowd of barbers, waving old-fashioned clippers which glinted in the sunlight. There were one or two children, dressed in exceptionally baggy trousers, who were flying little blue kites in the air. Voldemort Omar didn't seem to be anywhere to be seen, and as for the loads of angry mullahs he had expected, they seemed to have melted into thin air.

And so Johnny marched on, dumbstruck. His huge green anorak seemed to weigh down on his portly frame, and he felt peckish. Nevertheless, he couldn't help noticing about three thousand cheering Tajiks and Uzbeks mobbing him enthusiastically, and tugging on his dark blue, bullet-proof vest. The ground was very dusty indeed, as if someone had been pounding it with a giant hammer. There were mysterious stains on the road, and many of the houses looked smashed to pieces.

"Hello," said Johnny, clutching his wizard's videophone in one hand. "Er... I'm from the BBC, and if it's OK, I'd just like to do an interview." A great mass of gesticulating figures in ragged tunic surrounded him, and hoisted him with almost no difficulty on to their shoulders. Someone pulled a bottle of pumpkin fizz from Johnny's pocket, and waved it wildly.

"We had better get cracking," whispered a Welsh voice in Johnny's ear. It was Hewdwig from The Six in London, and he was due on air at any moment. But there was someone else tugging at his trousers.

"The Six can wait," said a rusty, offhand voice. "First you must come to the Palace of Kabul."

Johnny heard the great cheers as he was carried forward into the remains of a throne-room. And then a shadowy figure stepped forward to greet him. "You are Johnny Simpson, I think," remarked the figure. "You have liberated our great capital, and it is time for your Ultimate Test. We wish you to unite all the warlords and every ethnic group in our battered country. The Northern Alliance can wait."

Johnny felt faint, and reeled back. He rubbed his eyes vigorously.

"Yes, Johnny. We want you to be King of all Afghanistan, to put together a peace-keeping force, and to form a coalition government! Will you do it?"

Johnny nodded his head solemnly. Yes, he would.

"But who are you?" roared Johnny suddenly.

"You will find out," replied the figure, who was slowly bursting into the most astonishing blue-green flames, "in the next broadcast!"

I'm A Literary Celebrity – Get Me Out Of Here!

for ANITA	for BERT	for BILL	for COLE
09011 3232 01	09011 3232 02	09011 3232 03	09011 3232 04

for DYLAN	for EMILY	for MRS G	for SYLVIA
09011 3232 05	09011 3232 06	09011 3232 07	09011 3232 08

for TOM	for VIRGINIA
09011 3232 09	09011 3232 10

Jungle. 7.00 a.m. In the presenters' eyrie.

DEC: Morning! It's Day Eight Of *I'm A Literary Celebrity – Get Me Out Of Here!*

ANT: And some of our ten writers have got cramp after yesterday's group task.

DEC: Tom Eliot's feet have started to pen-and-ink.

ANT: And Emily B is still wuthering away. She's used two narrators, and she's got a cracking title.

DEC: What's that then?

ANT: *Cathy Come Home.*

DEC: That's a play, isn't it?

ANT: At this time of the morning, it's probably a breakfast serial. Let's have a look in camp, and see who's still afraid of –

ANT & DEC: Virginia Woolf!

Shot of camp

DYLAN: After the tum-grumbling, bowel-shivered night, hush as all the spring-heeled writers feather their quills with the scrawlings of dawn, and the dibbling of His Nibs in the jungle's fat-spit jangle. The girls are drooling over the cookpot cockcrow –

EMILY B: Ey oop! Who's let t'fire out?

SYLVIA: Why is it so cold? Are they embers? Of course, they are embers. I put my candied hand to the heat. I have simply let it out, like a sigh, like a dried tide.

BERT: I came down, down here to eat, in the long hot shadow, the long hot baking shadow of the eucalyptus, and the pot, the round and bulbous pot, is in gloom, a deep dark gloom that is not a gloom, only gloomier.

EMILY B: Ey oop! They's no tea in yon pot. Sithee, Sylvia –

SYLVIA: The moon is like a spoon, spun. I am no maid. So how should I boil up, boil up, boil up?

TOM: Only, there is water under that red rock.

13

EMILY: Ey flaming oop!

Back to jungle eyrie.

DEC: Oh dear, oh dear. I don't think they're pen-pals today, eh?

ANT: They've lost the plot.

DEC: Anyways. Yesterday, if you remember, Bill Shakespeare only won four stars in the Cyclo Drama Trial. He had to hang upside down in a croc-infested swamp, and every time he found a new genre, he had to ring his bell.

ANT: But Avon wasn't calling for Bill, was it?

DEC: It wasn't. He got the history, the comedy, the pastoral-comical, the scene individable, but he totally missed out on the others.

ANT: Tragical.

DEC: It was.

ANT: No, that was one of the ones he missed.

DEC: Is that right? We didn't do that in GCSE. Anyways, as a result, the whole camp went hungry.

ANT: They ate a dog, a horse, a rat, but they had no fool at all. Gooseberry fool, probably.

DEC: So, anyways. The Great British Public have been voting on who has to face today's Bush Tucker trial. If you want Anita to Loos, ha ha, just add 01. If you want Bert down the pit, add 02. If you want to Bill to swan about, add 03. For Cole Porter to be tops, add 04.

ANT: If you want Dylan to go gentle into that fly-infested bog, 05. To see Emily B baht 'at, 06. And if Mrs. Gaskell's your dizzee rascal, 07.

DEC: For Sylvia to be the bees' knees, 08. To see Tom under the brown fog, 09. And for Virginia to have a DOOM of her own, 10.

Ant and Dec start travelling across the bridge. Meanwhile, in camp:

TOM: A rat crept slowly over the vegetation. Wallala leia lala.

ANITA: So Bill only got four stars. So I said he was some bard. So we were very hungry.

BILL: My curses on this murrain'd patch of land! 'Tis but a stew, where cankers grow apace, and perfidy doth blight our corn the while. Where is yon (*bleep-bleep*) jakes? I'd one fell swoop.

MRS G.: I've been a busy Lizzie.

DYLAN: Listen. Under the brushbrown branches, the camp is bristling. The witchety grub, concertina-blowsy, is mulch-tang on the tongue.

ANITA: So I said it is a moth. And so he said not for three years. So it is a delicacy. So I was sick. So I got no stars.

BILL: Thou but repeat'st thy words, as 'twere a stylus, stuck in a fatal groove, and in such wise, that echo hath itself grown doubly dim.

COLE: It's de-bilitating, it's de-batable, it's de-lirious. It's box-fixated, intoxicated, approximatedly great – the way that salmon are sapped of stamina, and weighed by the gramme on a plate. It's de-meaning, it's de-ceptive, it's de-niable.

TOM: la la.

VIRGINIA: But of course, it will come to a conclusion, a close. And here, one supposes, in the waters, here in the outback, are the stars which will coalesce. Not to drown; to go under; not that. All this trial and test, exhausting, tiring, fatiguing; and oneself at the vortex, the centre, watchable. Not as one might watch oneself (for here one sees heaven knows what tribulations); but viewed, all the same. And being viewed, is that not to be subjected to the fuss, the delight, the exquisite disquisition of the infinite numbers of voices which surround one?

MRS G.: Here's Ant and Dec. They're not from the South.

EMILY B: Ey oop!

ANT: Good morning! Today's bush tucker trial is called Streams Of Unconsciousness, and the British Public –

15

MRS. G.: You're from the North, aren't you?

ANT: Mrs. G., it's not you. Cole. It's not you. Tom –

TOM: In my beginning is my ending –

ANT: It's not you. Bert – it might be you.

MRS. G.: I said, you're from the North, aren't you?

DEC: Mind, she's turning vicious.

ANT: Okay. Bert, the British Public have picked *you* for today's trial.

BERT: In my deep, deep heart, I knew. And then I did not know. And yet, in the deepest dark of the deepness, in the hot bowels, the white hot bowels of deepness, where Demeter and Dis illuminate their blue-dark darkness –

ANITA: And so I said it's Bert. So it is not me.

SYLVIA: I am ears, all ears, pink as the peony nymph. See, I flower.

DEC: In a few moments, the whole camp will be crawling with snakes. For every one that you whack with this stick, you win not only a star, but chapters in books by F.R. Leavis *and* Terry Eagleton.

(Bert seizes the stick and clobbers Ant and Dec to death).

BERT: And yet how foul, how foul and filthy and degraded I feel. And yet how elated. And I have something to expurgate: reality TV.

BILL: Pah! Fie upon 'em!

TOM: Shantih.

EMILY B: Ey oop! By the 'eck, I've finished t'book. Three volumes!

COLE: "*…unquiet slumbers for the sleepers in that quiet earth.*" You're the top! – you're a Brontë Sister. You're the top, you're by Buena Vista…

Roll credits

16

Coochi-coochi

By the supermarket trollee,
In an eezi-fold-up buggee,
Underneath a quilto-kumfi
Lay the sacred infant dribbling,
And he spoke the tongue of tinies,
Sang the tongue of Not-Yet-Toddler,
'Oba-gurgle, oogle-oo-goo,
Bubba-bubba, mummee-wah-whah,
Urkle-gobba, plugga-wagga,
Blubbli-obblah!' wailed the infant
Till his mummee, Mrs Buncer,
Plugged his cakehole with a dummee,
Dummee dipped in maple syrup,
As approached a gushing grannee.
Grannee exited from Tesco,
From the quik-food in the freezer,
Looked into the fold-up buggee,
Whispered 'Coochi-mudjekeewis,
Husa-booti fula-babba,
Izzaneetha spitta-dadda,'
Called him 'Coochi-mudjekeewis,'
Even though his name was Jason
(Full name Jason Kristin Buncer),
He who plucked away his dummee,
Blew the sacred wind upon her,
Sicked upon the avocado
In the Tesco bag of grannee.

Siegfried Sassoon: *'I knew a simple lager lout'*

I knew a simple lager lout
Who liked to turn a warning shout
Into a long, splenetic roar
When locked out by the force of Law.

In autumn, full of fizz and froth,
He ranted like a Visigoth,
And charged with all his shaven mates
At locked and bolted football gates.

His knuckles raw, his numskull cracked,
He fell when once he was attacked
By one who had not yet been barred
And flashed around his ID card.

You mindless mugs who pay to see
Some prat not worth his transfer fee,
Creep home, for you shall never know
The cell where youth and lager go.

A Valentine from Emily Dickinson

I give my Love - without a flinch -
The Diffidence - of Bloom
And hope - that He - in quick Response -
Will furnish - Me - the Same

Emollient - although I seem -
And not with Hope - Suffused -
Should he accept this flower now -
My Heart - this Fruit - 'tis Bruised

With Hope - Unfounded - I persist -
'Til Passion's Taste - is mine -
And though I may be - all too Plain -
Yet - be my - Valentine

Craig Raine in the delivery room

This child emerges slowly
like a raisin from a dead man's mouth,

wailing like a banshee on hot bricks.
The attendants stiffen

like hatstands. Their rubber gloves
stick to their hands like cellophane

on a long-lost lollipop.
The umbilical cord, a twist of pink liquorice,

is snipped by the haberdasher's scissors.
My tears are hailstones

hitting the instrument tray like stray silver bullets.
In the distance, my wife

wraps the baby to her like lambswool
discovered in a forgotten bottom drawer.

This child is still sticky:
it has swum five Channels, fully greased.

Applications to be Poet Laureate

1. Andrew Motion: *In Quiet Confidence*

The telephone rings. It is the palace
- *no, the prime minister, his voice bright*
as an old spark. And I must confess
I have been half-expecting him to write,

and I know, and he knows, and Ladbroke's knows
what line is being quietly plied.
I think he is inviting me to choose
to step in those open brogues. *On parade.*

So I answer, half-scrambling my words,
in a jittery sequence, a series of whispers
which sound like time-clocks or goat's beard
in a light breeze just before vespers -

so I tell him, which I will, you know,
what my decision is. *Yes, that's correct.*
I know exactly what I have to do,
and he explains what titles to expect.

I've been the odds-on-favourite,
and will not blench at it, nor take offence,
when offered, though I may say *Shit.*
Is that all right? I'll have to do it once.

2. Carol Ann Duffy: *Queen Time*

Butt of wine. Guineas. The sound of sabres
rattling like teeth in the cut glass by the bed.
You love the clunk of the funeral bell, flat,
as you answer the coded call. Ode. Dirge.
Epithalamium. Your voice cracks like plaster
when the tall orders arrive on the same day
while the rest watch telly. Princess Anne,
or is it BT's answering service? The Abbey?

Visit. Assassin. Bishop. You have the guts
to garter the knights, to slice open their visors
as if they were hiding pearls. The last rites.
The Charity Shield, the sweet FA . You dash
a brocade of words to a fax, and you leave
the new Pursuivant gasping. Your country looks
fast-forward to a past where the present time
rhymes. I need the work, boss. I want the sack.

3. Wendy Cope:
Laureates And Their Boring Manifestoes

I've offered to be the Laureate -
I think it would be a breeze.
There are lots of things to be sorry at,
But I'm fond of royalties.

With apologies to Thomas Hood

Ben Burglar

Ben Burglar was a petty crook:
  Great theft? He wouldn't risk it.
He nicked the ginger nuts from fêtes,
  Which really took the biscuit.

A small post office was a steal,
  And here he was the champ,
For when he stole their envelopes,
  He always left his stamp.

He also robbed a bakery,
  Yet bread he would not take,
But stole a slice of Battenberg,
  Which was a piece of cake.

Ben Ballcock

Ben Ballcock was a plumber's mate,
  To humbler jobs assigned.
His boss would quickly fix a tank,
  Whilst he would lag behind.

He burst out laughing when they came
  To fix the water main,
But cuts were in the pipe-line,
  And his job went down the drain.

23

Harry Pooter, Harry Pinter and Dirty Harry Potter

from The Diary Of Harry Pooter

OCTOBER 16. Ronald and I discussed the forthcoming game of Quidditch. This is a most interesting sport, and by-the-by I have been selected to play for the Gryffindor team. My motto is, A new broomstick sweeps clean, as I told Ronald. Following the exertions of flying, there will be a great feast, according to Madame Hooch.

"After the match," I told her, "we will be lighter." I could not help roaring at this joke, which I explained at length to Ronald. Hermione was rather testy when I repeated it to her. She looked at me, and suggested that, whilst they were drinking the winners' health out of *goblets*, I had better raise my *glasses*. I confess that I did not see what was so amusing. Short-sightedness is not worthy of jest. Walked away, and, feeling rather aggravated, turned my trunk into a lizard, which was so small that I promptly fell over it.

OCTOBER 17. Spent the afternoon learning about Charms, with Professor Flitwick. It is a capital subject. Whilst the others were levitating feathers, I endeavoured to make my shoelaces tie themselves. Wizardry is extraordinarily useful for such an important skill, and I fancy it will be immensely impressive once I have taught them not to tie themselves together. Received a severe bump on my nose.

OCTOBER 18. In the hall, Draco Malfoy most impudently accosted me at breakfast. "Pooter," he said, "you are a scarface." I affected not to hear him, although afterwards thought of a splendid retort. "If that is a *cutting* remark, then I heard what you *zed*." Unfortunately, it is now too late to make it. Consoled myself by teaching my owl some spells. To my horror, it turned itself into a hatstand.

from Harry Pinter and The Philosopher's Pause

I remember Hogwart's. Yes. I remember the stairs. Always on the move they were, those stairs. You'd take a left turn, a right turn, keep tight hold of your wand, oh yes. They had more flights than a bumble-bee at Bognor. And Quidditch. There was a game. I mean, don't talk to me about Bludgers. I seen them coming, mate. I seen them. *(Pause)* And there was this snitch, a golden one, real gold, with wings of silver. It was a golden snitch, all right. You'd get up on your broomstick, hands hard, the fresh air whistling past your ears, and you'd beat off those bludgers with a bat. More like a club, in fact, that's what. Marvellous. And then they would come out of the sun, dodging and ducking, looking for the quaffle, and minding those bludgers. My father used to.... play. Used to. He was a top class Quidditch player. Never without a sniff of a snitch. A sniff. *(Pause)* You going to eat that pumpkin, then? *(Pause)* Yes, Hogwart's was all right. There were dragons, and ghosts. I'm not saying there weren't dragons and ghosts. I mean, I used to get up in the morning, put my glasses on, and rehearse my curses. You had to have a curse. Or a charm. I mean, you have to have the best charms. Never without a good charm, in case of Volde... *(Pause)* I once saw a unicorn. *(Pause)* And I was invisible, they couldn't see me. Not a bit. I wore this cloak, see. To find the stone. It was an invisibility cloak, and it made me... invisible. My mother gave it to me. Or made it for me, anyway. But that doesn't matter, it doesn't matter at all. Because I know his dark arts, dark as they come, very dark indeed, that's what. *(Pause)* Hogwart's. *(Pause)* I don't look like a wizard in daylight, do I?

from Dirty Harry Potter

Harry looked down at the snivelling troll. He was the kind of punk against which Dumbledore had been warning him. A mean one. The creature was quivering with silent intent, and a horrible slime flowed slowly from his jaws across the coffee-splashed linoleum.

Harry's face was a frozen mask. The lines on his face looked as if they had been etched in by an expert, and the quiff above his forehead was as still as an old potion. This troll wouldn't even have been accepted in Slytherin. He wasn't worth a cheese Quaffle. But he was terribly dangerous, nevertheless.

He let the scowl hang on his lip. His face looked faintly bemused, as if Snape had let him off a detention. The patches on his Hogwart's blazer were dulled and worn.

"Well, look," said Harry, "I know exactly what you're thinking. How many spells did he cast today? Was it six charms or only five? And was the Latin correct? Well, to tell you the truth, I've rather lost count myself. But being as this is a holly wand with a phoenix feather, eleven inches long, the most powerful wizard's wand in Hogwart's, and would turn you into a dumpling, you've got to ask yourself one question: " 'Do I feel lucky?' Well, do you, punk?"

The troll made a tiny motion.

"Go ahead," said Harry coolly, his expression unshifting. "Make my house point."

Celebrity Christmas

1. Delia Smith: Preparing The Bird

So, the Christmas dish we're going to prepare is a really brilliant meal, with a lovely English pedigree, and I want to kick off by sort of showing you the ingredient. And first and actually most important is the Canary itself. Now you will need a cage for this first. But it needn't be a terribly big one, because it won't actually be *in* there very long, although metal ones are the best, and not clear plastic.

Canary, which the Spanish call *Canaria* in fact, is very much better if we buy a male, *because* the males are the ones which sing all those lovely songs. So I want to show you a male canary, here it is, very yellow and seasonal, and the first wonderful thing you should notice about it is that its beak has been tied absolutely shut. For this you need just a lovely strong elastic band, and although I've used a jolly festive red one, a good old-fashioned brown one will of course do.

When I was scuffling on the terraces at Carrow Road last week, I was asked, how would you prepare a Canary? So, first of all, here is a cleaver. This is a really brilliant kind of a cleaver, which just slashes anything straight through, and if I had Gary Rhodes here, which I actually do, he's the dessert, I would obviously saw clean through his foul, disgusting, scrawny neck. But some people do say about Canary that *wringing* its neck just a little bit is the way to do it. Personally, I think a good old chop is best, and I always give the bird a lovely, extra sort of minute or two, taking the band off, to let it sing.

So. Here we go. One wallop, and we'll see just a little bit of blood, and that's a good Christmassy sign, because it does mean that the canary was lovely, pure and alive, and now it's a kind of really brilliant sort of dead. So, here's my pot, decorated with holly, and it's very important that it actually fits in, so let's have a bash. Excellent. It cooks in its own wonderful juices and feathers, and anyone who thinks I am prim and proper, cop this. Recognise these greasy spikes? Yes. So I call this next dish my Gary Baldy Christmas pud. It is a bitch to make, but I am a pretty horrid bitch myself.

2. Ainsley Harriott: Ready Steady Wrap

Yeah, okay, it's miraculous midnight, it's Christmas Eve, and the coast is Clare, ♪♪ *whoooooo*, and there's no-one around but me, so I get hold of my nuts, *mmmmmmmm* thank you, nothing like cracking your nuts when no-one's looking! No time like the present to wrap up a present, ♪♪ *the presents are reQUESTED whooooooo*, okay, larvely, here's the sack of goody goody goodies, let's have a little peek, oooh, what are they like? Trust me, ♪♪ *I've got the wrapping paper and I'm gonna have a GOOD time yeah*, okay, come on, what we got. Ooh, fabulous-dabulous, check it out, *mmmmmmmmmm* time to get on the job, as we say (oooh!), and it's out with Percy Paper and Santa Sellotape! Fantastic! Let's perk up the packaging! My fingers are itching, ooh what are they like! Where have they been?! ♪♪ *We're gonna wrap it up awopbopalulaaaaaa* Cordear.

Okay, wozz this, I'm gonna show you how to jazz up some *mmmmmmmmmmm* fabtastical tasty little parcels AS QUICK AS A FLASH. Owright. Now this is all the lovely ingredients you need to make a very nice little present, very nice indeed, and what have we got ♪♪ *We've not got a lot but look what we've got*

Excellent, we have a special box, very nice indeed, and paper, I'm using some baking parchment, so the prezzie won't stick, larvely, this one's really flying now, some clear sellotape, that's nice - notice that, everybody, not that shiny Christmas sticky tape, and some ribbon, very smooth, you see, feel that? Absolutely. Smooth. I like it smooth all the way round, way-hay-hay, what am I like? And a tag, lovely, and just a touch of very flimsy, almost see-through tissue paper for underneath, I like a bit of see-through underneath, oooh! Okay. Fan-tastic.

Now, lovely, twenty-five seconds, ladies and gentlemen, sharp pair of scissors, and just cut along the line of the paper, larvely, leaving plenty of edge, then scrunch up that tissue, fantastic, so the box has a wrinkly-crinkly look about it, one tiny strip of sellotape just to keep that tidy, then pop it into the paper, and fold left over right over left. ♪♪ *Holding and folding* Fantastic. A sliver of sellotape, little tip from Ainsley, score round the roll with a stanley knife first, then peel off the strips and stick-stick-stick it round the edge. Dab on a tag, larvely, and write *To My Darling Clare With Love From Your Lovely Ainsley* Absolutely brilliant. Little bow of ribbon to top it off. Mwah mwah mwah. Ooooh lovely nice wrapping, I could cuddle meself, just one thing, I forgot to put a present in. Oh no! Terrible!

3. Simon Schama: A History of Christmas

The traditional English (or British) Christmas begins like some squalling infant at 730, when the canny chef first navigates his way into the larder of destiny. And it's there that we find the first exotic trinket on the chain of the day's memorabilia. The cook confronts the turkey (which has been doubly stuffed) and the cat that, so the chronicler tells us, has been cooped up with temptation for a fraction too long. By 920, while the family is finishing off the Danish, this dodgy mog has been airbrushed out of the tale. In his sacred robe, the ritual pinafore of humiliation, the kitchen king-for-a-day has cut his losses and imposed a pretended purity upon the partly-nibbled gobbler.

But 1030 is a much more significant moment in the studied autonomy of the chef. Missing implements - knives, carvers, skewers - resist his self-righteous belief in his innate ability. Search high, search low - and the head of the British (or English) household yields to no-one in his capacity for searching - and it seems that everything is doomed to disaster. And by 1125, a new regime has been imposed.

The key question, in fact, of 1125 (unlike 920) concerns the actions of the wife. It stamps her mark. By 1202, much of the husband's quondam authority has been stripped, stropped, reversed with clinical precision. The turkey, like the self-styled head of the household, gets it in the neck. By 1335, both are basting at top temperature, and the knives are out for the whole family. She has asserted her authority, and in the engine-room of British (or English and Scots) history, she has roasted the hot political potatoes. It is the reign of the tantrum.

When 1501 arrives, there is a temperamental assault on the dignity of the top table. In a wintry atmosphere, the principals meet, it is said, with a vengeance. But the family is not to be thwarted. Parsnips are buttered and browned. Sprouts, scrounged from a Tesco bin, are cut with the ubiquitous cross (he likes his veg, does the timorous tyrant, who once boiled an artichoke in a fantastical pan). Cranberries fizz like martyrs.

Between 1553 and 1635, England is once again a buzzing hive of exasperated anticipation. A pantechnicon of comestibles makes its way to the well-scrubbed trestles. And by 1649 - so our history defines it - the blades will be sharpened, and a new course will be taken up by puritan enthusiasts.

4. Charlie Dimmock: seating the guests at Christmas

Righty-ho, now if you've got a table for twelve, basically you want to be puttin' any old aunts (*tantinabula senilibus*) at the far end, so they give each other a bit more protection, which creates this really nice natterin', and it's also quite a good idea to keep them in the shade, because tantinabulas like a really good drink, but not much feed. You got to keep the kiddies (*excitatio childrensii*) outdoors till the very last minute, so they don't go nowhere you don't want. So we've dotted them either side of Grandad (*awkwardea cussis*), right over from the teenagers (*spottiche dysfunctionos*), they've got quite a pungent smell mostly, and you have to basically really tie them together, because they've got aggressive root systems, and they're often too big for their boots. All right? Yeah. So what I want is a proper old Dad, you got one of them, come on, show some enthusiasm, I want this one (*pater beerissimus*) right up the end. You're going to have to really push this one, otherwise it's going to droop right over, all right, sunshine? Right into that seat there, and don't forget to keep it tanked up, so it can cut quite a few slices from the bird, it can be quite a big flowery thing, because if you put a scarlet hat on it, it can be a really key structural feature. Fantastic. Do you want to theme your siblings (*sororii hectica*), because I like keepin' them together, okay, it keeps the blues from spreading. Well then, there's your brother-in-law (*unfuni jocus*), if you tuck him in near the pater, that creates a fabulous vista up through the candles. So is there enough space for you (*matrix frazzlea*)? How do you fancy a little bit of a seat here, near the veg, that's ideal for things like this. You're going to have use a fork occasionally to make sure there's a spread of stuff about the place, and keep your eye on the awkwardea, is he a special favourite of yours? If you want it a bit more variegated, you can always make two more little spaces, and push in a couple of neighbours (*nexdorus frugali*), does that inspire you to start diggin' in? We can chop and change a bit, shift the sororii round a little, and then weave the neighbours in and out of the table-legs. There, that's really fabulous.

5. Kurt Cobain's Christmas Journal

I tried putting the lights on the tree for oh, about 35 minutes. Ive totally vowed Ill do it. The lights are on a long lead that encircles & loops the viridian spiky needlesome hyperhigh pine. So I have literally been walking strolling round the tree then found Ive walked one way and then back so when I basically get back to the start its still on the ground and wrapped around my feet. Well I wish I knew someone who could help me because, uh, it doesnt work. Its kinda hard to play these corporate macho materialist consumerist games like putting these flashing flickering lights on a tree. I wish there was a tiny elf to cum & help me.

Things to do thru christmas
1 Get a hold of selotape
2 Ring all the pukey & trash filled journalists whos minds are basically self hipnotized
3 Practice making cheesy dips & other gunk

Im not in too hip on christmas. This is not a statement of phony anti fascist overexageration. This is not white, male, corporate vomit. This is not sacrilege, lets face it. I mean, this world totally talks shit about fairys on the tops of trees instead of things like: rabid, overhyped, pissy, mall-going, baby boomer hypocrites, licking their dollar bills with, uh, self opinionated toungues, when their basically giving in to the notoriously crass intimidating corporations. Gee, Ive been so long writing this the christmas cookies will be burnt to cinders. When you take a lot of heroine you are basically fucked up if you try to cook 4 calling birds, 3 french hens, 2 turtles & the other thing, nevermind. Once I saw Santa Clause in a chesnut puree.

Difference, indifference. I like the raw sunset on snow. I like smashing up store windows. I love the promise land of a childs eyes. Hey cheer up, yeah sure why not, I may feel like a dork, but if Ive got 250 lights twinkling on a tree like superhypermost stars, it will be the epitomy of our morals if weve made it a crusade. OK dude. Its kinda like the totally familiar realizations of what happens when you check into alternative christmas punk rock reality and it doesnt suck.

On A Plate
Ill heat this up its like a bird
I pricked the skin now the juice is clear

The head is gone no wattle splayed
In my dream it walks away

Chorus   Wild turkeys goose is cooked I know
            its dead before I looked

I burnt my fingers so their crisp
So what the hell if I eat your kiss

Its on a plate Im in a state
I must repeat am I in a state?

When Courtney comes back, uh, I will not be freaked out. She will take me like a wild swan, uh, up into the clean & precious & basically sensitive & unretarded universe. And she will feed me this indescribably sweet booze which is whoa! minty, and is called creme de monthe. Smells like green spirit.

6. Edwina Currie's Christmas Diary

December 25

Oddly enough, I think sprouts are terrific. Why would you want to have carrots? That you would find a hard question to answer, I bet. Spent an hour this morning just weighing the sprouts up in my hands, thinking, these should steam well. Wish I could handle sprouts as firm as those every day of the week. B liked his sprouts well-done, God bless him. I had to show him how to take them into your mouth while they were still firm. I do find men are a bit slow about sprouts. Would I want them all mushy? No, thank you.

Anyway, I like to peel away the outer layers. Sounds like a big effort, doesn't it? Well, I think the preparation is more than half the fun, and the slower the better. If you give a chap a sprout - or a savoy cabbage - they take off the leaves in no sodding time. They haven't a clue. You feel like saying, Hey, chum, that's a marvellous vegetable you have there, you have to treat it with a lot of respect. In fact, when you take the knife to a sprout - and lots of other girls have said this - you should cut a little cross on the end. Not that B would have pooh-poohed this. Maybe he would have come over and rinsed them. Oddly enough, he

33

was quite like a sprout himself. Very tactile. Perhaps a bit green.

I come from Liverpool, and I was chairman of housing in Birmingham. And so that brought me into plenty of contact with sprouts, thank God. By the time I was a junior minister, I had been dealing with sprouts for 17 years. I was better known in the country than anyone except Margaret Thatcher, and even she wasn't marvellous with sprouts. Something to do with Brussels. I do find that peculiar.

My new husband, John, is an absolute rock. But even he is so bloody amateurish when it comes to sprouts. I've told him to toddle along, God bless him, and bring me a gin. He says that he prefers parsnips. Gadzooks! Well, I suppose they are also marvellous vegetables, and maybe I'll bloody well butter them for him. Anyway, I do still feel pretty fed up about B. Wish I could have been offered a parsnip by him. Boy, that would have been terrific. Did I ask? Of course. He held my hand (what did he expect me to do? Pop a dollop of mashed potato on his tongue?) and said he could have offered me a reasonably decent leek. I was livid. But oh, I did think about him with my sprouts in his fingers, warm and sticky.

But perhaps we would have got careless. And could I ever have prepared Christmas dinner for him? I bet that would have been impossible. Anyway, oddly enough, I have moved on now. There are plenty of vegetables in the rack, and I have a marvellous new chopping-board. So do I still hanker for B? A bit. Another sprout, perhaps?

Ted Hughes looks in the mirror

My eyebrows are as thick as thieves.
They hang like shags of tobacco
Above a nose like a wedge, a doorstop.
They could probably get knotted.

A chin juts out. A blunt,
Almost pointless boulder of bone,
Stuck out stern from the face.
The lips are as grim as poachers'.

Curving quietly, up to no good.
The furrow between them is rough:
They seem to snag on laughter.
Nothing much given away here.

And the hair, thick as quills
From which feathers are stripped:
Swept back by an oily rake.
There is great weight on my forehead.

Dylan Thomas looks in the mirror

In the pudgy summer of face
Where in flesh moulded dough of quick thickening chins
Kneaded and knocked into place
Gaze dog squatting eyes in fissures
Pinched by cold
Snubbing boneless nose under pressures
Of white and larded temples stropped old
As the edge of hair thins
Or scrummages on skull's crinkled heath,
Ears like curl handles of cup
While mouth pouts and its spout of steam
Glazes bone china teeth
In skin of sickly cream
And the nostrils tip
To whey the roly-poly of infant fat features
And eyes sullen and blithe alive as little leeches.

Milked skin slack-happy over skull's repose
And under the watery dewlap of face
The forceless nose
Pug nostrils wide like railrunning tunnels
Lord it over fished lips
And lump chin.
Here is the ebbed recessional of hair
With barroom stare
And pin-
Backwards of curl ears like potato chips
Whilst sunk to the gunwales
Of throat are my tremulous sprung-voiced
Words with which in tongues I am hoist.

Bob Dylan:
Stuck Inside Of Fern Hill With The Ocean Blues Again

Oh, the young man plays whistles
Round about the farm
I'd ask him about his chrysalis
But I know he feels no harm
And the daisies and the apples
Sing with the streams and sheep
And the stables fly to paradise
Whenever he's asleep
Oh mama, can this really be the end
To be stuck inside of Fern Hill with the Ocean Blues again?

Well, the foxes bark their praises
And the cock does sing his hymns
And you feel the spinning place is
Where Adam stretched his limbs
But Time flies by so sudden
And he drowns me in his sea
Though underneath these iron waves
I sing my melody
Oh mama, can this really be the end
To be stuck inside of Fern Hill with the Ocean Blues again?

George Formby: *When I'm Teaching Drama*

Now I go drama-teaching
To earn an honest bob -
For a nosey parker
It's an interesting job.
It's a job that just suits me,
A drama teacher you would be
If you could see what I could see
When I'm teaching drama.
Assemblies take place in the hall,
I'm at the head man's beck and call,
I haven't got a room at all
When I'm teaching drama.

    In my profession I'll work hard
    Until my wages freeze -
    You haven't seen an ad, have you
    Which reads 'Incentive Es'?

Here's forty kids to exercise,
The room is half the staffroom's size,
But then I'm trained to improvise
When I'm teaching drama.
The parents want their Christmas fare,
For annual plays I must prepare,
This year I think I'll put on *Hair*
When I'm teaching drama.

    In my profession I'll work hard
    Until I'm out my tree,
    And when my nervous breakdown comes
    I'll teach them all R.E.

The other staff on me are hard
Because, despite my union card,
They think I wear a leotard
When I'm teaching drama.
My mind is full of teaching ploys
Of ways to match up girls and boys,
But heads say there is too much noise
When I'm teaching drama.
The order they think I dictate
Is "Come on, be a teapot, mate" -
In fact I tell them "Be a plate"
When I'm teaching drama.

> In my profession I'll work hard
> To pacify each kid,
> But should you see me on the street,
> Please, guv'nor, spare a quid.

I'm not a Mrs. Heathcote man,
I'm no Viola Spolin fan,
I simply do the best I can
When I'm teaching drama.
I give them skills to deal with life,
I help to sort internal strife;
Evenings I beat up the wife
When I'm teaching drama.
There should be brain behind my face
But have a butchers in my case
And then it's time to Find A Space
When I'm teaching drama.

> In my profession I'll work hard
> To teach my drama class,
> Despite them thinking I don't know
> My elbow from my head.

When the kids don't push and shove,
That's called interaction, guv,
Two fingers up means Peace And Love
When I'm teaching drama.
My work has got a social goal,
And all my pupils play the role
Called How To Make the Best Of Dole
When I'm teaching drama.
I don't think that I'm in the core
Curriculum, I'm out the door -
Does that mean I shall break the law
When I'm teaching drama?

> In my profession I'll work hard,
> I'll do it every day -
> The value of my subject's high,
> Though not, alas, my pay.

It's a job that just suits me,
A drama teacher you would be
If you could see what I can see
When I'm teaching drama.

from Enid Blyton's *The Iliad*

"Hey there!" shouted Hector, not looking very friendly. He walked over to where Patroclus was trying to run away.

Patroclus was quite cross, too, but, dear me, it *did* hurt *so* much! That nasty Euphorbus had got Patroclus in a dreadful fix by putting the spear through him.

And what on earth do you think Hector did? He went and stuck HIS spear into poor old Patroclus, too!

"Ooooh!" said Patroclus, and fell over.

"It serves you right," said Hector. "You shouldn't have tried to steal our nice town."

"It's perfectly horrid to stab me," wailed Patroclus. "You just wait till Achilles hears! You just wait!"

"Bother Achilles!" said Hector, and pulled his spear out. It was a lovely spear, made of shiny bronze.

And Hector snatched Patroclus's helmet - which belonged to Achilles! Oh dear - Hector *was* naughty!

Hector felt proud, but Antilochus ran to tell Achilles. He was quite out of breath when he got there.

"Well, I think it's JOLLY UNFAIR," said Achilles. He went into his tent, feeling so upset that hot little tears ran down his cheeks.

But never mind, Achilles! You'll get your own back soon, won't you? I expect you will!

That Famous Old Limerick By Lear

AND it came to pass that there came into that region a
  stranger saying, I have strange powers as to the
  healing of the sick;
2 And the name of the country from which this stranger cometh
  was Deal; and Deal was the name of his birthplace.
3 And behold, this stranger intreated the people and said, Lo, I am
  from Deal, and my powers are passing strange.
4 And the people asked him and said, What are thy powers? And at
  this the man of Deal goeth into a deep trance.
5 And he lifted up his eyes and saith, Behold, there is no such thing as
  pain; and moreover, I believe not that such a feeling existeth.
6 And some of the people marvelled at this, saying, Truly, this is a
  miracle.
7 And others murmured and said unto him, Peradventure thou hast
  about thy person a pin.
8 And the man of Deal answereth unto them, saying, I have.
9 And he taketh a silver pin in his hand saying, Behold; and he sticketh
  in the pin.
10 And the man, who was of Deal, crieth out as the pint entereth his
  leg; and these were the words of his cry: *Oblimeh Orileh*, which being
  interpreted meaneth, It hurts me.
11 And yet the man of Deal telleth the multitude, Although it
  appeareth that the silver pin hath caused me much anguish, yet is it
  not so;
12 And then the man of Deal saith again, This sensation cometh from
  my imagination, and it is not real, although it disliketh me.
13 And at this the people were sorely troubled.

The Big Read

David Beckham: Gulliver's Travels

Reading-wise, I have always had a favourite, you know, it's really good, actually, it's called Gulliver, Gulliver's Travels. Erm, and he has four of them along the way, four travels. And I don't know how he done it, it's amazing really, he gets to this place Littleput, and the people there is, erm, all little, size-wise. So, he's really big, and they're only about six inches, which is sort of very small, and he's like Michael Jordan, only a lot bigger, actually, and, they have this emperor. To be fair, there is a lot of, a lot of arguing, obviously involving the little people, and some of them has high heels actually, and some of them little heels, which is very, very funny, and this Gulliver bloke, erm, he's sort of like a really cool bloke, oh yeah, they tie him down with strings attached. That's like football, really. And honestly, adventure-wise, it is quite a big adventure. Oh yeah, and he has three other travels, one where he is the small one, like the one the crowd make fun of. And there is one place they get sunlight out of cucumbers, honestly. And one where the people is horses, and the others is dirty beasts. Yahoo. No, that's their name. So personally, I would, erm, vote for that. Gulliver's Travels. Which is by Gulliver, obviously.

John Prescott: The Turn Of The Screw, by Henry James

This is a book, and I'm not saying it isn't, which quite honestly has a speaker, very feminine, and she troubles herself with ghostial events, this is in Sussex, and she has employment as a governess to Miles and Flora, which is all well and good, teach as you would be taught by, which is her preposition to the unfurling of events in the house, a great house, but at the end of the day, which is twilight in my book, she has a habit of seeing dead people, and she suffers from insomniacs. And these dead people, I'm not saying buried, they pop up, okay, when she is least expectation of it, lakeside, through the windows, all very baffling, but what I am saying is this is a book which in bafflement keeps you guessing, no doubt, there's no doubt about that. So I say, which is a recommendation, a recommendation I recommend to you, that nothing is quite what it isn't, and I believe that this is the book you should read, sometimes the sentences are quite complicated, very complicated, but never mind, and what is a ghost story without ghosts, which keeps you guessworthy all through, so keep reading, which is my advisory, and no mistake.

Madonna: Mr. Peabody's Apples, by Madonna

Yeah, I love this idea, you know, physically, emotionally, it's kind of serendipity, and it's based on the Qabalah. It's £12.99. Thank you for asking me, I have to go now.

Tracey Emin:
A History Of The World in 10½ Chapters, by Julian Barnes

This is art, definitely. What happened, right, is they gave me this book to interpretate, and I thought, I'm out of here, because, you know, this is just another book, and who needs it, right? But the way he's fucking bisected this into ten, and he's still got this half a bit over, that's brilliant, because there's loads of people that would have called it eleven chapters, and it was like Boom!, you know, like, Ohmigod, that's quite unique! Boom! And you can't just look at it, right, you have to read it and come up with different pustulations about its meanings. And there is definitely stuff in there which is honest, right, like you wouldn't credit, only you have to. Like the moon, and Noah, and terrorism, which is a bit off, if you ask me. And love, definitely. Also it came with a free picture, which is all about painting limbs and things, right, sort of plasticination, only nineteenth century. You definitely have to read it, all the words there are genius.

Tom Paulin: Mr. Mean by Roger Hargreaves

I think this novel is absolutely tremendous. Really, it's a very powerful statement of that niggardly, miserly tradition which goes all the way back, right back to Milton in actual fact. I mean, when you consider all the bloated, smug, self-satisfied, middle-class pilfering of popular culture that masquerades as literature, then I think that Hargreaves is absolutely on the ball. There's something Bunyanesque about this novel. It has a quintessentially parsimonious take on the nature of what it actually means to be a miser, which is a kind of utterly radical irony. Quite frankly, I'm surprised that anyone could mistake the sheer Puritan quality of the writing, which is not in the least bit factitious, and which has a positively incantatory rhythm. Metrically, it has the same sense of frustrated grandeur that you find in Yeats. This is not some tinpot, gimcrack, faux-naif piece of flat-headed prose. It's very lively indeed. I mean, just listen to the incremental serendipity of the eponymous character's journey. This is a character who achieves the semi-mystical stature of Heathcliff, for God's sake. And the pictures are utterly delightful, too. There is a certain sanctity about the whole endeavour, if you know what I mean. I mean, we all know what Mr. Mean means, do you not think?

Margaret Thatcher: Ulysses, by James Joyce

May I just say that this is set in one day - one day! - in Dublin, and moreover in the Dublin of Homer, of the Greek poets? You tend to think of Dublin as quite, quite Irish, you know, whereas this is a tremendously long novel, you see, and that is why it is so complicated. If one reads it, one realises how tough life is, how hard. So look, just turn the pages with very great sorrow, and very great dignity, and - may we be frank? - just follow the words, and read Joyce. Read Joyce.

from *King Lear: the musical*
with apologies to Sammy Fain and Paul Francis Webster

Calamity Regan

Goneril: Liza Minelli
Regan: Doris Day

(at the end of Act I scene i...)

Goneril: We must do something, and i' the heat. (*Exit Goneril*)

Regan: Oh we're dead good gaugin' the state of our pater's brain:
He's a chatterin', batty an' flattery-courtin' insane -
Now is the hour - no time to delay -
Take his kingdom away, kingdom away, kingdom away!
Oh he's dead wood and he's definitely over the hill,
And although we bicker we're finally out for the kill -
Look at his Foooooool, his pet popinjay -
Take his kingdom away, kingdom away, kingdom away!

We'll change our evenin' gown
For his crown
With our royal embargo
On his Fool's farrago, that's our ploy, boy!

Oh we're fed good lines by that beddable Edmund churl;
He's a bastard boy but an earl for a go-getter girl -
It's in the stars, we'll wed, so they say -
Take his kingdom away, kingdom away, kingdom away!

The wheels of fate go round,
We'll be bound -
Can't you hear that drummin'?
Dire times are comin' down your way, hey!
Oh if Ed should wage a war on his pea-brained Pa,
He'll find he's blind if he thinks Ed won't get far -
The Gods may be odd, but who needs to pray?
Take that kingdom away, kingdom away, kingdom away!

In traducin' Gonerilla
When she's busy in a tizzy then I'll kill her:
She is strictly a non-starter
And she'll make an easy martyr
When the British people hear my latest line -
I'm glad to say she's got terrible friends of mine!

Why go stay with the folks a daughter loathes?
My beau says Nature's our design -
I know, it's time that Dad said Adios -
Yellin' like some whinin' child of nine!
Here's to leavin' no more botches,
And for little sis it's time for buenos nochas -
We cannot afford Cordelia,
Father's favourite lobelia -
When she'd nothing left, she couldn't but decline -
I'm glad to say that her future depends on some
      terrible friends of some friends of mine!

It's a dead good age when you're young and your Dad's four score,
And at eighty, Pater, what are we waiting for?
Listen here, Pa, you old so-and-so -
Get up and go, get up and go, get up and go -
Get up and gooooooooooooooooo!

Subterranean Homeless Blues

Compassion fatigue was said to have set in during the Rwanda massacres.

Johnny's in the government thinkin' 'bout the citizen
We're on the television seein' if he'll let us in
Man in a smooth suit/ voice fruit/ face fraught
Says we're all in bad shape/ need escape/ pass port
Look out kid Don't matter what they bid
Sod's law when but they're bound to try again
We better jump on the six o'clock
Lookin' for a new trick
The man in the frame game claims we're 'sick'
Ten million watchin' We'd better act quick

Maggie came hotfoot/ voice full of jackboot
Talkin' to the sick but sounded like a Queen Tut
Johnny says that any vote's worth the price of creosote
Even pay a nanny goat if you get to stay afloat
Look out kid Don't matter where we're hid
We better join the freakshows/ Strike a neat pose
For those who speak prose/ lookin' through our windows
You don't need a stethoscope
To diagnose their sucrose

Aaah play dead/ loose skin/ livin' outa dustbins
House of tin/ face thin/ with a photogenic grin
Typhoid/ typhus/ anythin' to make a fuss
In the dust/ Say You must make a front page outa us
Look out kid We're worth a few quid
To boozers/ bleeders/ tabloid readers
Reachin' out to feed us
The man in the peak cap's lookin' for a cheap snap
Headline and the leaders
Tell you how he freed us

Get born/ look forlorn/ listen what the hack says
In a mess/ abscess/ we could pay his taxes
Lie still/ don't shift/ don't ignore a horse gift
Twenty weeks of shelling and they put you on an airlift
Look out kid They're liftin' the lid
Better be an example just in case they trample
Grain of rice/ plague of lice/ looks as if it's ample
Wanna be relaxin'/ better not have black skin
A stump might work
If it dangles at an angle

from *Mr. Eurosceptic* by Roger Hargreaves

Mr. Eurosceptic was very, very sceptical.

Especially about Europe!

He was so Eurosceptic that he wouldn't put French dressing on salads. He wouldn't drink Irish coffee. And he wouldn't go to Dutch auctions. AND he wouldn't light a Roman candle!

Mr. Cash gave some money to Mr. Eurosceptic.

"It's good British money," said Mr. Cash. "It'll make you wealthy and healthy."

Mr. Eurosceptic was happy to be safe from all the nasty diseases abroad.

But one day when Mr. Eurosceptic woke up, he was covered in spots.

Lots and lots of spots.

Do you know what they were?

German measles!

Billy Bennett rewrites T.S.Eliot's *Ash Wednesday (part II)*

'Neath a juniper there's sat three dalmatian kind of cats
Feeling cool because they've left my guts for garters -
They've scoffed livers, legs and ticker and they've ate my
                              brain (don't snicker),
And who's to say that wasn't just for starters?

Then God, who cuts the mustard, said "Look here, these bones
                              is busted,
But that doesn't mean they're dead as dodo birds:"
So my skeleton (a goner) piped up "Hallow The Madonna!"
And blew kisses to the desert and some gourds.

Now a Lady in a shift, if you get my bit of drift,
Was the inspiration of this bony bunch;
Bits for which a cat won't whistle, like the nerve-ends
                              and the gristle
Seemed to sit up in the sand-dunes after lunch.

"If you want to say a prayer, leave the Lady over there,"
Said His Holiness, "and tip the wind a wink,"
So the bones got up a tune like a grasshopper in June
And what they chirped was really rinky-dink.

They sang all about a Rose which was lovely in repose
Even though it was as knackered as a surgeon;
They sang Love Is Really Rum and Each Time You Speak,
                              You're Dumb,
But they also blessed the Garden's Holy Virgin.

'Neath a juniper there's bones singing "Leave us on our own,
For it's peaceful in Sahara when you're scattered;
Here's a little lump of land, and you're welcome to the sand,
But we're singing psalms like nothing really mattered!"

51

The Trial by Richard Brautigan

Two men came into my bedroom. One was carrying a second-hand shadow. It looked like it had been folded by a chimpanzee.

The other man had a face like a holster.

"Listen," said the first man, sitting on the eiderdown. His voice was like a whisper which has had sandpaper rubbed on it. "We don't mean to be unpleasant. It's just a job we have to do."

"Oh," I said.

He put the shadow on the bed. It lay there feeling sorry for itself. A shadow needs as much attention as a Persian cat, but this one was sadly neglected.

"Are you O.K.?" I said to the shadow. It shrugged.

"We don't really enjoy it at all," said the second man. "But we'll have to ask you to get up, be accused of something, be tried for it, and, finally, be executed for it."

"We don't know why," said the first man. "We really don't."

"That's O.K.," I said. "I could do with excitement."

"Wear the shadow if you like," he said.

I tried it on. It was snug, like an old Indian poncho.

"How will I die?" I asked. It interested me.

"Like a dog," he said.

"Thanks," I said.

An Idle Boast *(after 'Banjo' Patterson)*

I've drunk toddies, tequila and Tizer
  In the taproom at Clacton-on-Sea;
I'm the bastard of Wilhelm the Kaiser
  By Rosie O'Neill of Tralee,
And I've called Rupert Murdoch a miser
  In the middle of afternoon tea.

I've lost count of the rhinos I've ridden
  On the banks of the Oxus by night;
I discovered where Lucan was hidden
  (He was parked in a barque in a bight),
And I found fifty quid in a midden
  After painting The Marble Arch white.

I was triple jump champion of Turkey
  In a fez that I filched from a Greek;
In a hospice in old Albuquerque,
  I was clinically dead for a week,
And I introduced Pinky to Perky
  While I practised the art of batik.

T.S. Eliot at Budleigh Salterton

At Budleigh Salterton
I can connect
Nothing with nothing

Hoowooh Hoowooh puffpuffchuff

Dr. Beeching, railway wallah,
Came too late to cut its station

April is the cruellest month, according
To Hector The Inspector, taxing
The pound in your pocket, stirring
Dull thoughts of spring rage.
Summer surprised us. It was hot.
We were in a Virgin, immaculate,
Hurtling towards the skirts of London,
Its postal districts packed like squares of wheat.
ON BEHALF OF VIRGIN, WE WOULD LIKE
TO APOLOGISE FOR YOUR PROMPT ARRIVAL

haha

The unbearable lightness of being
Only five stone six. When you came back, late,
From Paddington, my nose ran,
My blood boiled, I was neither living nor deaf,
Barely daring to breathe or achoo.

Faber the Publisher, some decades dead,
Produced some brilliant stuff, you know.
One is always smaller by not standing. Still,
Seated in heat, holding an ice-cream
Drip drop drip drop drip drip drip

And now, and again now, and now
All we want is a limousine.
What you want buses for if you can catch trains?
(About suffering, they were never wrong,
The timetable makers. 7.41.
Change at Worthing. But there is no
Train from Budleigh Salterton today.)

shunting shunting shunting

Harold Pinter: A Bear Called Paddington

Henry Brown: Where you from?

Bear: Peru.

Henry Brown: I knew a bear once. He came from Peru. Well, just out of Peru, it was. Yes. He had a llama, this Peruvian bear, a terrific spitter, what a spitter. (*Pause.*) What part of Peru, then?

Bear: Darkest.

Henry Brown: Darkest. (*Pause.*) Dark...est. (*Pause.*) How much more marmalade you thinking of scoffing, then?

Bear: Just... a few jars.

Henry Brown: You know, I bet you're a devil for buns. Sticky ones? Yes. You probably had more cream buns than a Lima llama on Bank Holiday.

Judy: Cut it out, Dad.

Henry Brown: Cut it out, what d'you mean? He comes here, big label round his neck, big label, says he's got an Aunt Lucy, what about Aunt Lucy, then? Come on, where's this Aunt Lucy? She was a goer, I can tell. (*Pause.*) This isn't Peru, you woolly git. It's Paddington.

Bear: Paddington. That's... that's a good name.

Sylvia Plath: Song of Myself

The moon is my medicine.
See, I lick her spoon
Clean as a whistle.

My light simply dribbles
From the worn scrawn of her lips.

Dribble, dribble, drab.
My fingers scribble,
Scratching at her lunar surface.

There are no craters on me.
My face is smooth.
Smooth as moon-milk in a pitcher.

Currents worship me.
They lay cold surf like turf at my toes.

I am marble or alabaster.
And my dark side is very dark indeed,
Black as a lump of cut coal.

Clive James: The Turm Of The Screw

Mrs. Grose was doing the wackiest impression of gobsmacked flummery since the first Philistine spotted Samson testing the temple pillars for strength. She had the sick look of a camel on the wrong end of some rubberised spittle doing its first return journey, and a mouth so open, you could have parked the Last Night of the Proms in it. A glint spingled in her eye, the size of a bad orange.

'Quint!'

A hint of Quint in an old bint's glint is bad news for a Norland novice with knicker neurosis. It hit me below my belt, and kept travelling. I'd thought the spick slicker with the frisky red whiskery was either auditioning for a West End walk-on, or fingering the local windows prior to a swift sales-pitch for double-shutters.

'Quint?'

Mrs. Grose, whose planetary presence somehow justified the music of her ample name, was still packing her verbal bags when I passed over my question. As repartee, it lacked a certain originality, but if I was a nut, there was no space for sledgehammer riposte. If the woman had beans to spill, you had to have the sauce to hand, and I had kegs of ketchup ready.

'Quint!' she cried. 'His valate!' The words fell from her palet like tiny malates and smasheroonied their way through my skull. 'He's dead,' she added.

Dead! So she was speaking of a spick spook! You didn't have to be a barmy-boots to feel a cold mitten squeezing your shriek-box. I let out a fresh yelp. I hadn't come to Bly to be banjaxed by peeping paedophiles with a phantom penchant for canny nannies like yours truly.

King Lear: the limericks

Goneril/Regan: Pop's tops!
Lear: Cordelia?
Cordelia: Oh, *Dad*.
Lear: I banish you!
Kent: Gad!
Lear: Vanish!
Fool: Mad:
        Believe me, these sisters
        Deceive you.
Lear: The twisters!
Gloucester: And my boy's a bastard.
Edmund: Too bad.
Edgar: I'm disguised. Tom's a fruitcake.
Lear: Me too!
Goneril/Regan: Prise those eyes out.
Gloucester: I'm blinded. Boo-hoo!
Edmund: I fix my own odds.
Gloucester: The gods are such sods.
Edgar: No they're not. Jump! All right?
Gloucester: And that's true.
Regan: My hubby's just snuffed it. To bed!
Edmund: My lady?
Goneril: He's mine!
Albany: You're still wed.
Lear: The law is an ass;
        Forgive me, my lass.
Cordelia: Of course!
Regan: Ugh!
Goneril: Agh!
Edmund: Ooh!
Albany: They're all dead!
       Good old gods! Three cheers!
Kent: I feel queer.

Lear: She's dead. Howl. Fool. Gurgle.
Albany: Oh dear.
Kent: He's dead, and I'm dying.
Edgar: It's time to start crying.
          I'm king. That's your lot. Shed a tear.

John Betjeman: Return To Slough

Oh borough of Slough, oh borough of Slough,
How graceless and tasteless my poem looks now:
A pox on me now, bless your fresh cotton socks,
And your crisp Orange Pippins, created by Cox!

Like you, I embraced what was strictly commercial,
And gazed at the skies like your William Herschel:
In Slough he found Uranus, a planet one cheers -
And you've also made Mars Bars for eighty odd years.

Queen Victoria rode her first train from your borough,
And your trading estates are as large as they're thorough.
Slough's Sinkins produced Mrs. Sinkins's Pink –
O Slough, how my verses were not worth their ink.

Oh borough of Slough, oh borough of Slough,
My graveyard in Cornwall prepares for your plough –
An importunate poet, I bathe you in praise,
And now you're made famous by Ricky Gervais.

Cilla by Samuel Beckett

To be born White, but Black there had to be, shadow falling, she was White, I was Black, cavern and darkness, she wasn't there, I was there, anyone could see me, anyone who had a heart, I had a heart, she had no heart, they were fab, they wrote for me, she didn't sing, couldn't open her gob, I opened mine, what's it all about, it was the end, end of my word for me, I had the voice, Black and no mistake, but they gave me the words, why me and not another, I took the step, step inside love, a fool am I, I was no fool, voice like a razor, I told them, she didn't have Bobby, I had my Bobby, but why not the girl next door, she was next door, I was the girl next door, but I was there, there and not elsewise, Black and not White, I was chosen, she wasn't chosen, I knew the questions, I gave them answers, didn't I chuck, but what of the future, come in number three, I'll be there, I'll be Black, she'll be White, I'll give the word, surprise, surprise, right between the eyes.